A Practical Guide To Focus Groups

Research and Evaluation Guides

by Sarah McNicol and Pete Dalton

2

A Practical Guide to Focus Groups Research and Evaluation Guides

Sarah McNicol & Pete Dalton

Layout Design: web-aviso.com

ISBN: 978-1-716-40929-5

First published December 2020. Evidence to Action

First edition

Contents

Introduction to the guide

Much of the research and evaluation we do combines academic understanding with more commercial approaches to research. These two approaches, academic or scholarly research and market or commercial research, are often seen as separate types of activity, but in these guides, we attempt to bring together knowledge and skills from both sectors. We recognise that each has its strengths, for example, academic research tends to be more rigorous, but market research is more practically focused. We're also aware that each approach has its weaknesses; for instance, academic research can be less accessible, while market research can overlook prior knowledge on a topic.

These guides, therefore, incorporate ideas from both forms of research – they are based on evidence from research methods literature, whilst also being practically-focused. They are intended as an introduction to research and evaluation for people in a variety of roles and sectors who may have limited existing knowledge or experience of research or evaluation.

Introduction to focus groups

This introduction to focus groups is intended for anyone with relatively little, or no, previous experience of running focus groups.

It starts by describing what we mean by a focus group and explaining when you might want to use one – and when not to. In the following section, we provide practical advice on questions like how to recruit participants; where and when to hold a focus group; how to run a group; ethical considerations; and how to make a record of what happens in a focus group. Following this, we outline alternative approaches you might want to consider, such as online focus groups, the inclusion of activities and other research methods that have similarities to focus groups. The final section of the guide offers tips, troubleshooting recommendations and case studies.

We hope this guide will be helpful if you are planning to organise your own focus group, or simply want to know more about them. If you want more information or advice about focus groups, do please get in touch via either www.evidencetoaction.co.uk or email info@evidencetoaction.co.uk

What is a focus group?

A focus group involves a small group of people (usually 6 to 8 participants) who are guided through a discussion on a specific topic by a moderator or facilitator.

Focus groups have been used since the 1940s and are now common across many academic disciplines as well as being a familiar method in market research. In a focus group, a group of people are asked a series of questions based around a fairly loose topic guide. The topic guide is not rigid, but allows for variation, for example, in the order in which questions are asked and the inclusion of additional prompts by the facilitator. This may sound very similar to an interview; however, focus groups differ from interviews because they are concerned with the interaction *between group participants*, rather than between the interviewer and interviewee. The emphasis in a focus group is on *group responses* and connections developed through the discussion, rather than insights or stories offered by individuals.

The facilitator, or moderator, of a focus group plays an important role, but it is a very different one from that of an interviewer. The facilitator's role involves ensuring the smooth running of the group; managing group dynamics (e.g., encouraging everyone to input ideas); introducing relevant themes, questions, or ideas at appropriate times; and making sure the discussion progresses in a way that will help to meet the research or evaluation aims.

Why use a focus group?

Focus groups can help you to better understand communities' needs, preferences, or priorities. Their strength is in supporting the types of tasks that are usually best undertaken by groups. For example, you can use focus groups to generate ideas; to explore a variety of different issues or perspectives; and to test solutions. A focus group can help you to learn more about the concerns within a particular community and allow you to use this information to guide future action. Some examples of potential uses for focus groups include:

- to gather background information about an issue

- to generate and develop ideas (which can then be tested further through other research methods)

- to encourage creative participant-led solutions

- to explore complex ideas and behaviours

- to gain more in-depth understanding of data gathered through other research methods (for example, to explore unclear or conflicting survey responses)

- to gather user (or staff) impressions of a service, organisation or institution

- to identify potential barriers or problems with a new service or programme

- to prioritise specific areas in which there is a need for action

- to test potential solutions to problems.

A note of caution: It's sometimes argued that an advantage of focus groups is that they can shift the balance of power from the researcher to participants. As the emphasis is on the interaction within the group (rather than between the interviewer and interviewee), it's argued that focus groups allow participants to have more control. While this can certainly be true, it's important not to assume all focus groups will automatically achieve a significant redistribution to power. In a more traditional focus group model, the researcher or facilitator still retains a high degree of control, deciding on the time, location, length of the focus group, group composition, questions asked; and when to move the discussion on. Section 4 includes some approaches that help in ensuring focus group participants can have more control.

When not to use a focus group

While focus groups are useful in many situations, there can be occasions when they are not an appropriate research or evaluation method. For example, focus groups are not ideal tools for capturing the views of a wide range of individuals since the sample size is usually very small and selective. Equally, they are not suitable if you are interested in individual experiences and stories.

Focus groups *can* be used to explore sensitive topics, but in this situation a lot of care needs to be taken especially around group composition and establishing ground rules.

We don't usually advocate focus groups as a means of reducing research costs. Focus groups are sometimes are argued to be more cost-effective than interviews, but this assumption needs to be treated with caution as when you take account of preparation and organisation time and possibly higher room hire and refreshment costs, the difference in cost is likely to be much less than it might at first appear. Transcription costs for focus groups are also greater than for one-to-one interviews.

Using focus groups alongside other methods

In many cases, focus groups won't be the only research or evaluation method you use; it's common to combine focus groups with a variety of other methods. The following are just a few examples. You might use a focus group:

- to confirm or develop what you have already found through desk research (e.g., academic literature or policy documents)

- to explore findings from surveys or other methods in greater depth (for example, to explain conflicting or unexpected responses)

- to identify important issues that can then be explored further through surveys or other large-scale studies involving a larger group of people that is more representative of the population.

- to provide feedback on initial findings or suggested solutions devised through other methods to gauge reactions from communities affected.

In these examples, methods are being used sequentially (one after another), but you might also use focus groups concurrently with other methods, for example, to collect data from a different group of stakeholders. An example of this is using focus groups to collect data from young people alongside interviews with their teachers.

Focus group practicalities.

Having explained what focus groups are and when they might be used, this section describes the practical issues to consider when arranging a focus group.

Recruiting participants

Focus groups usually involve 6 to 8 people, but they can be smaller or larger (between 4 and 15 people).

The composition of the focus group will depend on the aim of the research or evaluation. There is a lot of conflicting advice about how homogeneous a group should be: for example, should all group members be the same gender or ethnicity, or is it better to have a mixed group? It's impossible to give a simple answer to these sorts of questions as it depends on what questions are being asked and what is likely to work best for different communities. To some extent, this depends on the topic you are asking participants to discuss. For example, for certain health issues, it may be best to run separate groups for men and women, but in other cases, this may not be necessary. It's also important to remember that the characteristics of the facilitator (and notetaker) can also be a significant factor that affects the running of the group and how open participants are likely to be: e.g., are they linked to the community, or an outsider?

When you're recruiting focus group participants, it's important that the individuals you invite are comfortable as a group and feel they have something in common, such as sharing a common experience. However, for a useful discussion, you also need to try to include participants who hold a range of views on a given topic. Balancing the degree of similarity and difference between participants to ensure a successful focus group can be tricky, and often a factor you have limited control over anyway.

Something else to be aware of is the possible differences in power between participants. For example, bringing together management and front-line staff in a single focus group may have benefits in certain circumstances, but in many cases is likely to mean front line staff feel less free to express their opinions and concerns.

Focus groups participants are normally recruited by convenience sampling (an example might be anyone attending a mother and baby group on a certain day) or purposive sampling. Purposive sampling involves recruiting participants who meet certain pre-defined criteria (for instance, having a baby aged between 6 and 12 months old).

There are a number of ways to recruit focus group participants. Often, the easiest way is to **identify an existing group** to serve as your focus group (if one exists). This might be a community group, a youth club, a staff committee etc. This approach is likely to involve working in partnership with external organisations that can help you to gain access to the group and explain the value of your research to its members.

Ready-made groups have the advantage that participants already know each other and are likely to feel comfortable with each other. They are also likely to have a designated time and location that is convenient for members to meet, so you're not asking people to make an additional, and possibly inconvenient, trip. However, using an existing group may mean all participants do not meet your ideal selection criteria and, in some cases, may have their own ways of interacting that are not best suited to a focus group discussion (e.g., a formal committee).

A slightly different way to recruit participants is to work with an external organisation (or a 'gatekeeper') in order to recruit from a wider group, they have access to. For example, you might approach a headteacher or head of service who then asks for volunteers from amongst their students or staff or suggests individuals who may be willing to take part. This means you can ensure that everyone in the group meets your selection criteria.

Another possible way to recruit participants is through **contacts from surveys or interviews** conducted earlier in the research or evaluation project. These individuals might be invited to a focus group to allow them to expand on views they expressed or to help to develop solutions to issues raised.

If you are running a series of focus groups, **snowballing** can be a useful method to recruit participants. This means that people who have participated themselves suggest acquaintances who they think might also be interested in taking part.

Finally, on occasions, you may need to directly **advertise** for participants. This can be via a variety of methods depending on the group you want to recruit from (e.g., posters, social media, mailing lists).

It's usually a good idea to over-recruit to a focus group as often people have to cancel at the last minute or fail to turn up on the day. If you have recruited through an external organisation or existing contacts, invite around two extra participants. If you have recruited by advertising alone, it may be wise to invite three or four extras. It's a good idea to send the participants an email/message or to phone them a day or two ahead of the focus group to remind them of the date, time, and other important details, and ensure that they are still planning to come.

Arranging the focus group

Focus groups should be conducted in locations that are accessible; spacious enough for the group size; and convenient and comfortable for participants. When the focus group is a ready-made group, the most suitable location will probably be the place where they would usually meet as it's likely to be somewhere, they feel comfortable and are able to access easily. These are also key considerations if you need to find a venue for a focus group yourself. Ideally, the space will be somewhere that is familiar to participants. When this is not possible, it should at least a type of location where they are likely to feel comfortable; for example, a formal boardroom may feel intimidating to many people. There are purpose-built focus group venues with viewing rooms, but these are more expensive to hire and may not be as accessible (or familiar) to participants as a community venue.

The focus group venue needs to be accessible to participants – for example, not too far from their home or work - with good public transport links and/or parking depending on how your participants are likely to travel.

The room needs to be private and reasonably quiet, so the focus group can be conducted without distractions. Acoustics can also be important:

a room with a lot of echo can make it difficult for everyone to follow the conversation, and for a clear recording to be made.

In general, you don't need much equipment to run a focus group – simply chairs which are normally arranged in a horseshoe. A lecture theatre or classroom layout is not likely to be suitable unless it can be easily adapted to a more informal layout. A flipchart and/or whiteboard can be useful. If you plan to include any additional activities (see Section 4), you may need tables and sufficient space for the group to spread out to do these.

When planning your focus group, you should decide on a time that is most convenient for the participants and takes account of the daily patterns of their lives, for instance, that might mean avoiding school run times, or offering evening or weekend sessions.

A focus group typically lasts for between 60 and 90 minutes, but this can vary; for instance, if more interactive activities are used, it can take longer. The needs of group members can also affect the length of the focus group, for example, children or people with particular health issues may find it difficult to concentrate for longer periods so a shorter session may be more suitable.

Focus groups can be difficult to recruit for and you may well need to offer incentives. This might mean providing refreshments or offering a more direct incentive. Vouchers (e.g., for online shopping or a supermarket) are usually best as it means the facilitator doesn't need to carry around large quantities of cash. However, it's important to find out what type of vouchers are useful to participants; for example, there's no point giving vouchers for a particular supermarket if there is no branch nearby.

Depending on the makeup of the group there are other factors that may make it easier for focus group participants to attend. These might include refunding travel expenses (or if possible, pre-purchasing tickets for participants) if they need to make a special journey and offering childcare facilities (or a contribution to childcare costs) for the duration of the focus group.

Recording the focus group

There are several options for recording a focus group. You can choose just one of these, or use a combination, either as a backup or to record different aspects of the discussion.

Notetaking

Ideally a notetaker will attend the focus group alongside the facilitator, but for logistical, financial, or other reasons, this is not always possible, so the facilitator may have to make any notes themselves. Sometimes, the facilitator and notetaker may swap roles during the course of a focus group, so each leads a particular section of the discussion whilst the other takes notes. In addition to recording the main points of the conversation, the notetaker usually also captures other aspects of the session, such as body language and mood of the group.

In any event there are several options for notetaking:

1. Writing in a notebook that is not visible to participants during the focus group.

2. Observing during the focus group and making written (or audio) notes immediately after – this can be more acceptable in groups who may feel uncomfortable if they are conscious someone is taking notes of the conversation.

Making notes in a way that is visible to the group – for example using a flipchart to record the main points of the conversation. This can include words alone, or words and images that capture the key themes of the conversation (visual notetaking).

Audio recording

Audio recording is frequently used for focus groups as it allows for an accurate recording of the conversation – including quotes - and for most people it feels less intrusive than video recording. You might want to use more than one recorder depending on the size and layout of the room. Ideally, try to test the position of the recorder(s) before participants arrive.

The disadvantage of audio recording is that it can be difficult to identify individual participants in the focus group. Usually this is not a significant problem as you are more interested in group responses than individual ones. However, this can sometimes make it more difficult to follow the discussion – especially if the transcriber was not present at the focus group.

Video recording

Video recording helps to solve this problem as it is easier to determine who is speaking at any moment. However, for many people, being videoed can be off-putting and as a video camera (and tripod) is larger than an audio recorder, it's more difficult to 'forget it's there'. Also, depending on the layout of the room, it may be difficult to capture the whole focus group in the viewfinder.

On the other hand, an important advantage of video recordings is that they are able to capture not just the conversation, but also the body language of participants.

Recording body language

You can record body language if you are using a video recorder, or simply by notetaking.

Focus groups allow you to pick up on nonverbal information which may be important to your research (for example, excitement, doubt, hesitation, or stress). Often the way a response is given is more valuable than the response itself (for example, the impact of a long pause or reluctance to answer). Research suggests that only a fraction of our interpersonal communications is done through the words we say. This means that it's important to observe voice tonality and non-verbal communication where possible. This can include things such as changes in eye contact, physical movements, and posture.

Where someone gives a verbal response but makes a significant non-verbal response at the same time, this may point to a lack of congruence between what someone says and what they really mean and can provide a prompt to delve deeper into the response and seek clarification. While some non-verbal cues may have generally accepted meanings, for example, slouching, lack of eye contact or crossed arms may mean someone is disengaged or uncomfortable, it is important not to assume that is the case. People have their own unique individual motivations and reactions so someone may find sitting with crossed arms keeps them warm or slouching for them is a comfortable way to sit. Ideally, it is best to calibrate each individual i.e., notice how they are now and then notice when there has been a significant non-verbal change.

Regardless of the recording method used, if more than one person is involved in running the focus group, you should schedule in some additional time immediately after the session so that the team can regroup and share feedback. If the focus group is run by a single facilitator, it's equally important that they set aside time to reflect on their experiences of the group soon afterwards. These reflections can be helpful especially in the initial stages of analysis (see below).

Running a focus group

Focus groups rely heavily on the skills of the facilitator and these can significantly affect the quality of the data gathered. If you haven't facilitated a group before, it's a good idea to observe another group first, perhaps acting as a notetaker. Alternatively, you could co-facilitate with a more experienced facilitator.

Introduction to the focus group

At the start of the focus group, before you ask any questions, welcome the group, and introduce yourself and explain your role. Also introduce any colleagues (e.g., notetaker, interpreter) and allow them to explain their role in the focus group.

Ask participants to introduce themselves (usually first names only) – this often happens as part of an icebreaker activity (see below).

You can also give participants stick-on name badges to wear if group members do not already know each other.

If the focus group is an existing group who know each other well, you could still ask them to wear name badges for your benefit, or you can make a simple plan of the room and note who is sitting whereas they give their names.

Explain the main ethical considerations of the project and check that all participants have completed consent forms prior to the start of the focus group (see below). Cover any housekeeping matters (e.g., fire evacuation procedures for the venue) and then begin by recapping the purpose of the research and the objective for the session. You should check whether participants have any questions, either about the research overall or the focus group specifically.

The following are typical ground rules for a focus group that you may wish to share with participants. However, be aware that these rules may need to be adapted to needs of a specific group to allow them to interact as naturally as possible.

Example of focus group 'ground rules'

- Participants should speak one at a time (for the recording and/or note taker).

- Any views or opinions expressed during the focus group will be confidential and anonymised. Participants must respect this and not repeat opinions or experiences outside of the focus group.

- Participants should listen to each other and respect each other's views and diversity of opinions.

- They should share their views and experiences openly and honestly.

- The facilitator may ask them to move on to another question or re-visit a question according to the time available.

Icebreakers

An 'icebreaker' at the start of a focus group can help to get participants talking, especially in a group who don't already know each other. The icebreaker should be simple, fairly light-hearted and something that everyone will be able to answer. It's best to ask a very open question that participants can choose how they wish to answer, for example:

- Where is your favourite place?

- What's the best thing that's happened to you this week?

Asking more direct questions (e.g., How many children do you have? Where was your last holiday?) can lead to unanticipated problems for participants who do not have simple answers to these.

One way of running an icebreaker is to ask everyone to take a few M&Ms (or other coloured sweets) from a bag. Participants then share something on a given topic for each coloured M&M they have. The following list gives some examples of things you could ask for each colour.

- **Red:** Share something about your family

- **Brown:** Share something you are good at

- **Yellow:** Share something you have watched or listened to recently

- **Green:** Share something that you can't live without

- **Blue:** Share something that makes you feel happy

- **Orange:** Wildcard – share anything you want to

As an alternative to asking a question, you could do one of the activities in Section 4 as an icebreaker. This can be particularly useful when some participants are delayed or arriving at different times as it allows them to join in the activity as they arrive.

The topic guide.

A topic guide is a rough list of questions, prepared ahead of the focus group; it is usually divided into themes. The purpose of the topic guide is to loosely structure the focus group and lead the discussion as naturally as possible. Focus group guides typically include 5 or 6 broad themes, which may include a larger number of sub-questions. There is an example of a focus group guide in Appendix A. In the focus group, you do not need to use the questions in the order you initially planned; it is better to follow the natural flow of the discussion and introduce themes as they are suggested by participants' responses.

A good focus group topic guide will:

- explore mainly qualitative issues (asking what, where, who, when and how?)

- be open-ended and allow for in-depth responses (e.g., "What do you think about...?", "What was your experience of ....?")

- explore just one idea per question.

- where appropriate, take a chronological approach.

- typically begin by asking about positive experiences before moving on to negative experiences.

In addition, make sure the language you use for your questions is similar to that participants themselves would use. For example, don't include acronyms or technical terms unless you are sure the group will be familiar with them. Before the focus group, it's worth spending time planning how you might use follow up questions or prompts.

There are two main purposes for follow up questions in a focus group:

- to find out more detail or seek clarification (e.g., "Why?", "Could you give an example?", "Could you tell me more about that?" etc.)

- to ask for other views and alternatives (e.g., "How does everyone else feel about that comment?", "Does anyone have a different experience to that?")

If you are running a number of focus groups, you may need to adapt your focus group topic guide according to the specific makeup of the participants in each group, for example, to reflect issues in the locality where they live. You may also need to adapt your topic guide if participants respond in very different ways to those you had expected. If this happens, keep in mind the aims of your research, and adapt in the best way you can to achieve these aims, even if that means you deviate somewhat from session plan.

Ending the focus group

At the end of the focus group, remember to thank the participants for their time and participation and to let them know that you appreciate their contributions. You should also explain the next steps in your research and how participants will be informed of any outcomes that come about as a result of this focus group. You should also remind them of any admin tasks they need to complete, for example, claiming travel costs.

Analysis and reporting

There are many possible approaches to take when analysing focus group data. The data you have gathered may include a variety of qualitative responses including:

- Transcripts of focus group discussions

- Notes made by the note maker and/or facilitator.

- Reflections by team members made after the focus group.

- Additional data collected through focus group activities (e.g., flipcharts, photographs)

Analysing and reporting qualitative data.

The most common way to analyse qualitative data is through 'coding'. This involves categorising data according to themes or topics. These themes can either be determined beforehand (usually based on the research or evaluation aims or existing literature) or identified through reading the transcripts and other data after it has been collected. Often, researchers will use a combination of the two approaches. Coding can be done manually (using highlighters or cut and paste for example) or using software. As you develop your analysis, you may decide to combine codes and/or add new codes to reflect themes as they emerge from the data. The data included in each theme can include direct quotes from participants, as well as summaries of a discussion and the research team's reflections.

Once you have coded the data into themes, the next stage is to use this as a basis to write up the findings. There are many ways of doing this. You might wish to structure the analysis by answering the research questions; by combining themes into larger categories or topics; or by considering how your focus group findings compare to other data – from your own research or wider literature.

Feedback to participants

In addition to any reports, you might need to produce for funders or other initiators of the research or evaluation, it's important to think about how to feedback findings to focus group participants.

This might be through a short summary, infographic, or video for example. If you are working with (or for) an organisation that will make practical use of your research, it can be useful to work with them to provide feedback to participants not only about the research findings, but also what changes they will lead to.

Ethics

For some research and evaluation, you will need to gain permission from an ethics committee before you are able to collect data. This might be an external body such as an NHS Research Committee; your own organisation; or a funder or partner organisation. It's important to find out whether you need formal ethical approval at an early stage as you will need to factor time for this into the project planning.

Whether or not you need to obtain formal ethical approval, it's good practice to provide your participants with written information about your research or evaluation prior to them participating in a focus group (see Appendix C for an example of a 'participant information sheet').

This should be written in accessible language for participants and explain:

- exactly what they will be expected to do

- the fact that participation is voluntary, and they don't have to answer anything they are not comfortable about

- how the results will be used

- how data will be stored securely

- contacts detail in case of queries or concerns

- confidentiality and anonymity (for example, confirming that the discussion will only be listened to be the research team and any comments will be anonymised in reports)

- how to withdraw from the research if they wish (with a focus group, it is important to be clear that an individual can withdraw at any point by leaving the group, but afterwards it may not be possible for them to withdraw from the research as it's likely to be difficult to identify and remove an individual from the recording).

Additional to providing written information, it's advisable to repeat the points of the participant information sheet verbally prior to the focus group to check everyone has understood and can ask any questions. This is a chance to remind people that the discussion is confidential, and that nothing said in the focus group is to be repeated.

However, they should be aware it's impossible to guarantee that none of the participants will repeat what is said. Once they are happy with the ethical issues around participating in the focus group, all participants should sign a consent form (see Appendix C for an example). Participants are entitled to a copy of this form if they wish. Although the most usual way of obtaining consent is via a signed form, it is possible to do so verbally (and record this on audio or video) if this is more appropriate for group members because of literacy or cultural issues.

If you are carrying out research or evaluation with children and young people under 16, you will need to obtain consent from a parent or guardian as well as the young person themselves (the latter is sometimes referred to as 'assent').

For research with young people between 16 and 18, although it's usually advisable to provide information for parents, you can use your professional judgement to determine whether to formally request consent from them.

Focus group options & alternatives.

This section discusses options to consider if you want to move beyond a straightforward focus group. This includes using activities, running online focus groups, and considering some alternative methods to engage with groups.

Using activities in a focus group

In addition to discussing questions or themes, you may want to incorporate one or more activities as part of your focus group.

There are several reasons why you may wish to incorporate an activity:

- As an ice breaker (see Section 3)

- As a different method of capturing information (e.g., visual data)

- To break up a larger group and give everyone an opportunity to input.

- To avoid a few people dominating discussions

- To cater for participants who may be more comfortable doing something practical than speaking in front of a group.

- To provide a change of pace and variety for participants

- To give you space to reflect as a facilitator and decide on the next stages of the focus group.

The following are just a few examples of activities you could use. Some can be completed as a whole group, but alternatively you can divide the participants into several smaller groups. In the second option, each group can then 'report back' and discuss each other's responses.

Construction or collage

Provide participants with magazines or craft resources and ask them to create something that represents their response to a question or issue, for example, what they would like their community to be like.

Drawing

Provide participants with drawing materials and ask them to draw their response, for example, their experience of using a service. For some, a blank page can be daunting, so you might want to give more structure, for instance, a comic book style series of frames to fill, or even the start of a story for them to complete.

Thermometer

Draw a thermometer on a piece of flipchart paper and ask participants to write their responses to a question on post-its (e.g., Ideas in response to "How could this service be improved?"), then position these on the thermometer scale to indicate whether they are 'hot' (good or important) or 'cold' (bad or unimportant).

Target or web

Draw a target or spider's web on a piece of flipchart paper and ask participants to write their responses to a question on post-its and position these on the on the target or web, with the most important/best being near the centre and the least important/worst being towards the outer edge.

Standing on a line

This is a physical activity that can be done if you have a larger space. Mark a line, for example, by placing a rope on the ground or using the length of a wall. Indicate one end of the line/wall as 'agree' or 'good' and the other as 'disagree' or 'bad'. The centre of the line is neutral. Ask participants to stand along the line in a place that best reflects their response to each question or statement (e.g., "There should be more activities for teenagers in my community").

Metaphors

A common question in market research focus groups is to ask participants to think of a metaphor for a product or service, for example, what animal or type of car best describes it. You can use this approach for a variety of issues, not just commercial products. As an alternative to asking participants to describe their metaphor, you could ask them to draw it, or to create a sculpture (e.g., using Playdoh). This can give them more freedom to create unconventional or abstract metaphors.

Sorting, matching, categorising, hierarchies and establishing relationships.

There are a variety of activities you can do using flashcards with key ideas or options written on them. These can be pre-prepared by the facilitator and/or produced by participants during the focus group. You can ask participants to sort these into order (e.g., most important to least important); sort them into categories; or otherwise arrange the cards to help you better understand their views.

One way of structuring this is the Diamond 9 approach. In this, the group selects the nine ideas they think are most important, then orders these into a diamond shape with the most important at the top and the least important at the bottom. (See template in Appendix B).

Online focus groups

Improvements in technology mean that virtual or online focus groups have become more popular in recent years. Virtual focus groups can be *synchronous* i.e., conducted live in real time through video chat, or *asynchronous*, i.e., not in real time, for example through bulletin board groups or a forum that runs over a period of a few days. There are many options for online focus groups. We use Zoom (although this needs a pro subscription for more than one person over 40 minutes). Of course, if you are moderating an online focus group, it's important you become familiar with the software that you are using in advance.

Online focus groups can overcome geographical issues as participants are not limited to the pool of people who can easily travel to a physical location. They offer flexibility as participants do not need to travel and venues do not need to be hired. This means they can also be cheaper to run than face-to-face groups. In addition, participants may be more at ease in their own home environment. As with face-to-face focus groups, we find 6-8 participants tends to work best for online focus groups.

As software has developed, there is increasing flexibility in the way an online focus group is run. Sharing multimedia items is easy for example: images, video, whiteboard diagrams, audio and mini surveys are all possible, but make sure you load and test these beforehand. Most virtual focus group software allows for live group discussion, as well as sending individual chat messages to a moderator. The latter can be useful if participants want to share sensitive information. Communicating through a variety of formats is possible so you could consider mixing traditional verbal discussion plus chat functions and online polls. You can adapt many conventional focus group activities to an online experience, for example, you could use chat to emulate exercises such as brainstorming. You can also use online break out rooms where participants can be put into smaller groups for activities and the moderator can drop into monitor the progress of each group.

Online software offers functionality that can help a moderator to facilitate the group in ways that would be tricky to replicate in a face-to-face setting. Chat functions can provide a means of getting the moderator's attention and preventing more vocal respondents dominating discussions. This is useful because if visual cues are limited to a participant's face there are less non- verbal cues than in face-to-face focus groups. A further useful function is that most software packages allow for direct recording of the focus group and save details of chat transcripts.

Whist online focus groups can have many advantages, it's important to remember that participants need access to appropriate technology (i.e., webcam, browser, earphones, and microphone). It's possible this may exclude some potential participants who don't have access to technology. More broadly, online focus groups face technical risks for example, broadband and connectivity issues and local hardware limitations. Some participants may not be comfortable in an online focus group if they do not have good digital skills or are reluctant to appear on camera. It can be useful to allow some time at the beginning for people to settle in and get familiar with their online set up. If your software allows, provide participants access to the software before the group formally starts so that they can test their set up and ensure that it is working. In addition, participants may fail to turn up, or may drop out at the last minute, as they are less invested in the process than those who have travelled physically to attend a focus group.

A further consideration is that the choice of online focus groups needs to be suitable for the research topic. For example, if the requirement is to touch, taste or smell something this is not possible online. Anything that requires face-to-face physical interactions will not be possible, and this includes payment of any incentives for participation on the day.

Alternative methods with similarities to focus groups.

There are a number of research and evaluation methods that, whilst they are different from focus groups, have some overlap or similarities. We've included brief information about some of these here as they may be worth considering as an alternative to a conventional focus group depending on the participants you are working with and your research or evaluation aims.

Group interviews

Group interviews may appear to be very similar to focus groups (in fact, the terms are sometimes used interchangeably). In a group interview, people are brought together and asked a series of questions as a group. However, the key difference is that, in group interviews, the interaction is between the interviewer and participants, rather than amongst the participants themselves. Group interviews are therefore best used when you are interested in individual stories and responses. Group interviews are most commonly used with children, interviewed in friendship groups, rather than individually, to help them feel more comfortable. However, they can also work with other groups, particularly those who might feel nervous in an individual interview situation.

Photovoice

Photovoice was developed by Caroline Wang and Mary Ann Burris in the early 1990s. It uses participatory methods that encourage participants to lead the research process. It assumes that participants are the experts in their own situation. Participants are asked to take photographs around a research theme. They then meet to discuss the pictures they have taken. Whilst not strictly a focus group, this discussion session often has many similar features. The exact format can vary, but it usually involves participants sharing their images and explaining the stories behind them. The group then discusses the themes and issues emerging. Sometimes, groups make a collective decision about what images they think are most significant. Following the discussion, participants arrange to share their photographs and stories with policymakers or community leaders.

Nominal Group Technique (NGT)

Nominal Group Technique (NGT) is a structured form of small-group discussion that can be useful to gain a consensus on ways to respond to a problem or issue. It can help to balance the influence of more and less vocal individuals in a group. However, it often means a less in-depth group discussion so may not be suited to more complex issues and/or where more creative solutions are likely to be required.

NGT usually involves the following four steps.

- Generating ideas: The moderator presents a problem or question and asks each group member to write brief ideas or responses. Everyone does this individually, typically for 5-10 minutes.

- Recording ideas: The moderator asks each group member in turn to suggest an idea and records these on a flipchart to make them visible to everyone. There is no discussion at this stage (not even clarification). Individuals may pass if they have no further suggestions to offer. This continues until all ideas have been documented (or for a fixed period of time).

- Discussing ideas: Each idea recorded is discussed with a focus on its relative importance. The discussion may help to clarify meaning; explain logic or thought processes behind the idea; raise or answer questions; or indicate agreement or disagreement within the group.

- Voting on ideas: Group members vote privately to prioritise the ideas. Depending on the number of ideas (or solutions required), individuals typically rank what they consider to be the most important 5 or 10 ideas. These are transformed into votes (e.g., a score of 10 for the top ranked item; 9 for the second and so on) which are tallied to identify ideas rated most highly by the group as a whole.

Co-design workshop

Co-design enables users of a service, activity, or intervention to be actively involved in its design. Co-design workshops tend to be more hands-on than focus groups, for example, using collages, storyboards, paper prototypes or 3D models. In many cases, workshops bring together users with designers and other professionals on an equal footing to discuss ideas and design solutions to problems.

Troubleshooting focus groups

The following are some of the more common problems that can be faced when running focus groups, and some possible ways to address them.

Dominant personalities overpower and steer the group's responses.

- Give quieter participants a chance to contribute (look out for signs that they have something to say but avoid putting them on the spot).

- Ask questions that encourage other viewpoints (e.g., "How does everyone else feel about that comment?", "Does anyone have a different experience to that?").

- Introduce an activity that requires participants to work in smaller groups, for example, ask them to discuss a question in pairs then share their ideas.

Participants are reluctant to disagree with the dominant view.

- Introduce an activity that allows participants to express views individually or in pairs. Or alternative viewpoint ...

46

- Ask participants how they might react to this.

Some participants are reluctant to discuss sensitive issues.

- Carefully consider the composition of the group and how this may affect responses at the planning stage (this includes the facilitator and other team members who will be present).

- Inform participants beforehand about the topic they will be expected to discuss.

- Use existing groups or friendship groups where people may feel more comfortable.

Participants start to talk about issues not relevant to the focus group.

- Be careful not to decide too quickly that a discussion is irrelevant; it may be that the group has different experiences or a different way of approaching a problem from those you expected.

- If you are sure the discussion is moving too far-off topic, move onto your next theme or question (ideally one that is a clear break from the previous discussion).

The discussion becomes heated and the group is polarised.

- Defuse conflicts by moving the topic on (or parking an issue).

- Introduce a refreshment break.

There are practical difficulties organising a focus group (e.g. finding a suitable time and venue)

- Offer alternatives and run a series of smaller groups rather than one larger group.

- Consider online focus groups as an alternative.

Case studies

Case study 1:

Identifying priorities for recreational activities for young people

---

Background to the research

The aim of this research, commissioned by a youth support organisation, was to find out what young people thought about the recreational activities they were currently offered and what further activities they would like to see offered by the organisation.

Why focus groups?

We chose to use a focus group because the organisation commissioning the research was interested in how the young people as a group responded. Most of the activities offered were group activities (e.g., team sports), so the way in which the young people interacted as a group was central to the research. We also felt that young people may feel more comfortable in a friendship group than in an individual interview with an unfamiliar adult.

Recruiting participants

We recruited participants from existing members of the youth group, with the help of youth workers. This had the advantage of providing a ready-made group who were familiar with each other. However, we recognised that this meant we weren't including views from young people who would be eligible to attend, but currently did not. (This is something we probably would have tried to include in a larger project).

Location and filming of the focus group

We held the focus group at the location and time that young people would normally attend the youth group. This meant they didn't need to make a special journey or remember to attend at a different time than normal. The focus group was held in the summer when the group meets outside. We therefore held the focus group outside on an area of the playing field they use.

Format of the focus group

There were two part to the focus group. In the first part, they sat in a circle on the grass, whilst we explained what we were trying to do through the research. We then asked them to respond to a series of questions about the activities they enjoyed, why they attended the group, what they might change etc.

In the second part of the session, we did a series of activities. Given the topic being discussed, the makeup of the group and the fact that we were outside, we felt this was the most appropriate way to gather information. We asked several questions using the 'standing on a line' activity described in Section 4.

In another activity, we placed large coloured cards at points around the playing field. Each colour represented an answer to a question we asked. For example, for "What is your favourite sports activity from those on offer at the moment?", there were options such as red=football, blue=netball/basketball, green=cricket/rounders etc. When we asked the question, participants had to run to the card that represented their choice.

Recording the focus group

As we were outside, an audio recorder was unlikely to pick up much of the conversation. We therefore decided to make notes in a notebook during both the discussion and activities. We did this openly, explaining to the young people that we needed to make notes so we could remember what they had told us correctly. For the standing on a line activity, we took a photo of the group on the line (facing away from the camera) to get an accurate record of where they were positioned.

Reporting on the focus group

Following the focus group, we produced a report of the findings for the youth support organisation, plus our recommendations based on the data we had collected. We also produced a short bullet-pointed summary of the main findings for them to share with the young people who had participated.

Case study 2:

Exploring students' experiences of a university library service

Background to the research

The research was commissioned by a university library service. The aim was to gather in depth feedback from students with regards to the use and provision of library resources. The purpose was to aid understanding of the students' experience, to see what was working well and where improvements could be made.

Why focus groups?

Initially a feedback survey has been sent to all students asking for feedback on the library service. This provided predominately quantitative data with limited qualitative feedback. Focus groups were used to explore some of the topics identified through survey feedback and to investigate a selection of issues in more depth by drawing on mainly qualitative approaches.

Recruiting participants

The survey which had been conducted beforehand asked whether respondents would be willing to take part in further research on these topics and this included focus groups. It was made clear that this was optional and as a result, respondents were self-selecting. Those who indicated they would be willing to take part in further research were asked to provide basic contact details and the name of the Faculty and Department in which they were based. This provided a pool of potential participants for focus groups. From these contacts, a selection was invited to take part in focus groups. Selection was made with a view to represent students from each Faculty as evenly as possible.

Location and filming of the focus group

Six focus groups were scheduled. These were scheduled at different times and on different days of the week. This was done to ensure that students had the opportunity to be able to fit in attendance around their schedule of lectures or other commitments. Potential participants were asked to indicate which of the times that they could do and provide their top three preferences for dates and times.

Groups were arranged at three different campuses. This provided flexibility for participants to choose a location most convenient to them.

As most students tended to spend a lot of the week on campus and it was a familiar environment it was considered best to hold them on site.

Format of the focus group

The focus group initially took the form of a group discussion on a range of topics that had been identified from the survey. Each topic was presented in turn and feedback on it gathered from the group. Where appropriate, the findings of the survey were shared in order to stimulate reaction from the group.

At the end of the focus group, a list of possible improvements that had been identified from the discussion were drawn up into a list and participants were asked to allocate 10 points across these items using coloured sticky dots as part of a prioritisation exercise. It was recognised that this would not be an accurate exercise however it was useful to give an impression of where the highest priorities for improvement lay.

Recording the focus group

The focus groups were recorded using a digital voice recorder. This was placed in the centre of the table where participants sat, and an external omnidirectional microphone was used to enable all responses to be picked up. Two staff were involved in running the focus group, one to lead and facilitate the discussion and another to provide general support, to observe and to make notes of key points in a note pad. The handwritten notes helped to guide the writing up of the key points and identify parts of the audio which were most useful to focus on.

Reporting on the focus group

The feedback from each focus group was collated and analysed around each of the themes of the discussion guide, as well as any additional themes that had emerged during the focus group. Where there appeared to be specific issues of relevance to students in particular faculties or schools this was noted.

A formal report including a summary of key points was produced for library management. Also, a separate summary of the findings was shared with participants as well as within the university through channels such as a newsletter and intranet.

Summary

Ten Tips for Focus Groups

1. If possible, work with other organisations who have contact and credibility with the community you want to engage with to recruit participants.

2. Over-recruit for each focus group in anticipation of some drop-out.

3. Consider what incentives you may need to offer – or other factors that will be make it easier for people to attend (e.g., childcare).

4. Put participants' needs and convenience first when planning a focus group (e.g., choose a time and location that is easiest for them).

5. Pay attention to the way in which you greet participants and make them feel welcome. Make it clear that they are the experts, and you are keen to understand their views and experiences.

6. Make sure you are clear about any ethical procedures you need to adhere to at an early stage and factor this into your planning as this can be time- consuming.

7. Consider including an activity or alternative form of note making so you can capture data in different ways.

8. Be prepared to adapt and deviate from your plan if necessary, in order to best achieve your research aims.

9. Consider alternatives that may be better suited to your group if appropriate (e.g., online focus groups, co-design).

10. Plan how you will provide participants with feedback from your research and make sure you follow this through.

Further resources

Focus groups.

Center for Community Health and Development, University of Kansas, Community Toolbox: Section 6. Conducting Focus Groups

https://ctb.ku.edu/en/table-ofcontents/assessment/assessing-community-needs-and- resources/conduct-focus-groups/main

Gibbs, A. (1997), Focus Groups (Social Research Update)

http://sru.soc. surrey.ac.uk/SRU19.html

Harrell, M. C., & Bradley, M.A. (2009), Semi-structured Interviews and Focus Groups, RAND Corporation

https://www.rand.org/pubs/technical_reports/ TR718.html

Oxfam (2019), Conducting Focus Groups

https://policy-practice.oxfam.org.uk/publications/conducting-focus-groups-578994

Sim, J., Waterfield, J. (2019), Focus Group Methodology: some ethical challenges, Qual Quant 53, 3003–22.

https://doi.org/10.1007/s11135-019-00914-5

Smith, M. K. (2011), Using Focus Groups in Evaluation and Research
https://infed.org/mobi/using-focus-groups-in-evaluation-and-research/

UK Data Service, Focus Groups

https://ukdataservice.ac.uk/teaching-resources/non-interview/focus-groups.aspx

Other methods

Center for Community Health and Development, University of Kansas, Community Toolbox: Section 20. Implementing Photovoice in Your Community

https://ctb.ku.edu/en/table-of-contents/assessment/assessing community- needs-and-resources/photovoice/main

Liebenberg, L (2018) Thinking critically about photovoice: Achieving empowerment and social change. International Journal of Qualitative Methods *https://doi.org/10.1177/1609406918757631.*

McMillan, S. S., King, M., & Tully, M. P. (2016), How to use the nominal group and Delphi techniques. International journal of clinical pharmacy, 38(3), 655–62

https://doi.org/10.1007/s11096-016-0257-x

Service Design Tools

https://servicedesigntools.org

Varga-Atkins, T., with contributions from Bunyan, N; McIsaac, J; Fewtrell J. (2011) The Nominal Group Technique: a practical guide for facilitators *https://www.liverpool.ac.uk/media/livacuk/cll/eddevfiles/iteach/pdf/qui de_for_ELESIG_v1.pdf*

Glossary

Gatekeeper: an intermediary between the researcher and participants who may help to recruit participants (e.g., a head teacher, employer, or head of a member organisation).

Mixed methods: includes both quantitative methods (e.g., questionnaires) and qualitative methods (e.g., focus groups) in a single research or evaluation project.

Participants: people who take part in research or evaluation, for example, as interviewees, focus group members or survey respondents.

Population: the entire group of people you are interested in findings out about through your research (e.g., all students at a university, all residents in a neighbourhood)

Qualitative methods: methods used to answer questions such as 'why?' and 'how?', typically through open-ended and more conversational approaches.

Quantitative methods: methods used to answer questions such as 'what/which'? and 'how many/how much'?', typically through collecting numerical data that can be analysed statistically.

Sample: a sub-group of the population who are participants in your research. You can identify your sample in a variety of ways (e.g., purposive sampling, convenience sampling, random sampling, stratified sampling).

Appendices

Appendix A:

Example focus group guide.

This guide was devised for an evaluation project evaluating the use of a resource pack of books for school libraries.

Theme 1: The school library (15-20 mins approx.)

- What words would you use to describe the library? Write these on post-it notes and put them on a flipchart grouping similar words together) (e.g., welcoming, boring, fun, peaceful, noisy etc.).

  Follow up: why have you chosen that word? / Can you explain why the library is ...?

- What do you do in the library? And how often? (e.g., library lessons, other lessons, homework, reading, borrow books, computers, activities)

- How important is it to have a school library? Follow up: Why?

  Do all students use the library?

- If you could design your ideal school library, what would it look like? What would it have in it?

Theme 2: Reading (15-20 mins approx.)

- What words do you associate with 'reading'? Write these on post-it notes and put them on a flipchart grouping similar words together (e.g., fun, boring, hard, easy).

- What types of books do you like – favourite authors, titles, genres? Follow up: Do you like to read other things e.g., newspapers, comics, online.

- What types of books do you like least?

- Where do you find the books you read? (e.g., school library, public library, bookshop, presents...)

- How do you choose a book? (e.g., cover, teacher/librarian/friend recommendation, displays...)

Theme 3: Resource pack (15-20 mins approx)

- Have you seen any of these books before? (show the resource pack books to the group, allowing time to read the blurb etc.)

- If you've read any already, what did you think of them?

- Which books would you be most likely to want to read? Why?

- Which (types of books) are you least likely to want to read? Why?

- What other books (titles/authors/types of books) would you like to see included in this pack?

Appendix B:

Diamond 9 template

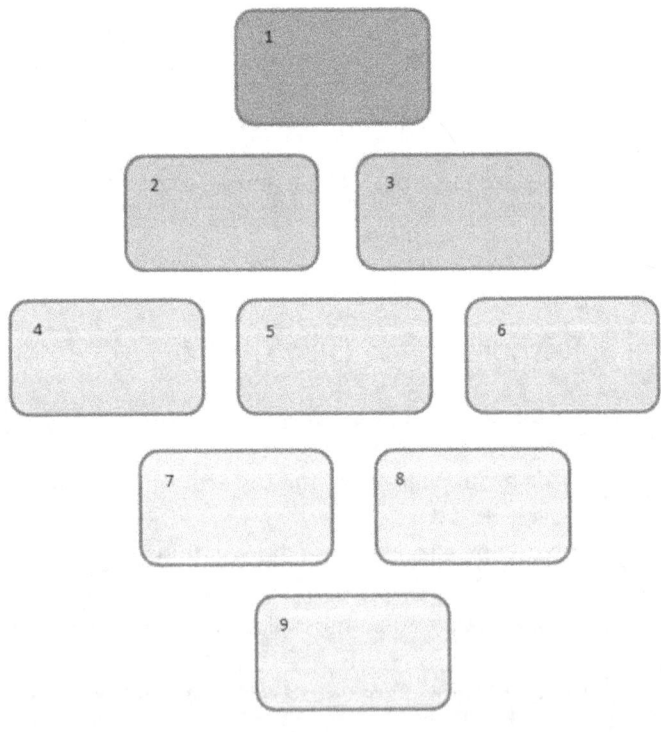

Appendix C:

Participant information sheet and consent form

1. Participant information sheet

INFORMATION ABOUT THE PROJECT

Provide some brief background to the research or evaluation project.

Explain who is funding the research/evaluation and who is responsible for carrying it out.

WHY HAVE I BEEN ASKED TO PARTICIPATE?

Outline the criteria you have used to select participants.

DO I HAVE TO TAKE PART AND WHAT ARE THE OPTIONS FOR WITHDRAWAL?

Participation is voluntary and you can withdraw at any point by leaving the focus group. However, please be aware because it can be difficult to identify individual contributions in the recording, anonymous comments you have already made may still be included in the research analysis.

What do I have to do?

You will be asked to attend a focus group organised and delivered by.................................

The group will last about. ..... hours and will involve approximately .... other participants.

The group will be asked to share views and experiences on a range of issues relating to ....

We will be taking notes/ audio/video recording the event and only the research team will listen back to   the recording.

Data protection & confidentiality

All information you provide will be securely stored on a password protected computer. No names or personally identifiable information will be included within the research process unless you specifically consent to this. Any personal and sensitive data (e.g., names, contact details) will be kept separate to all process data collected from the focus groups.

What will happen with the results?

Explain how you plan to use and share the results of the research / evaluation (e.g., reports, feedback to participants).

WHAT DO I DO IF I WOULD LIKE MORE INFORMATION?

If you have questions, you can ask the focus group facilitator.

Alternatively, you can contact:

[Provide contact details: name, address, phone, email]

Consent form

Thank you for attending this focus group which is part of the .... research/evaluation project.

- I confirm I have read and understood the participant information sheet and have had an opportunity to ask questions.

- I understand that my participation is voluntary, and I can refuse to answer questions if I want to.

- I understand I am free to leave at any time, but if I do, anonymised comments I have already made may still be included in the research analysis.

- I understand that all the information I provide will be treated in confidence and not shared outside the research team unless it is anonymised.

- I agree to notes being taken / audio recording / video recording during the focus group.

- I agree to take part in this research/evaluation project.

Name of participant --

Signature--

Date --

Name of researcher/facilitator --------------------------------

Signature --

Date --